Classic Car Show Adult Coloring Book

Preston Guymon

1932 Ford Roadster

1941 Willey's Coupe

1945 Dodge Rat Rod

1951 Ford Truck

1956 Bel Air

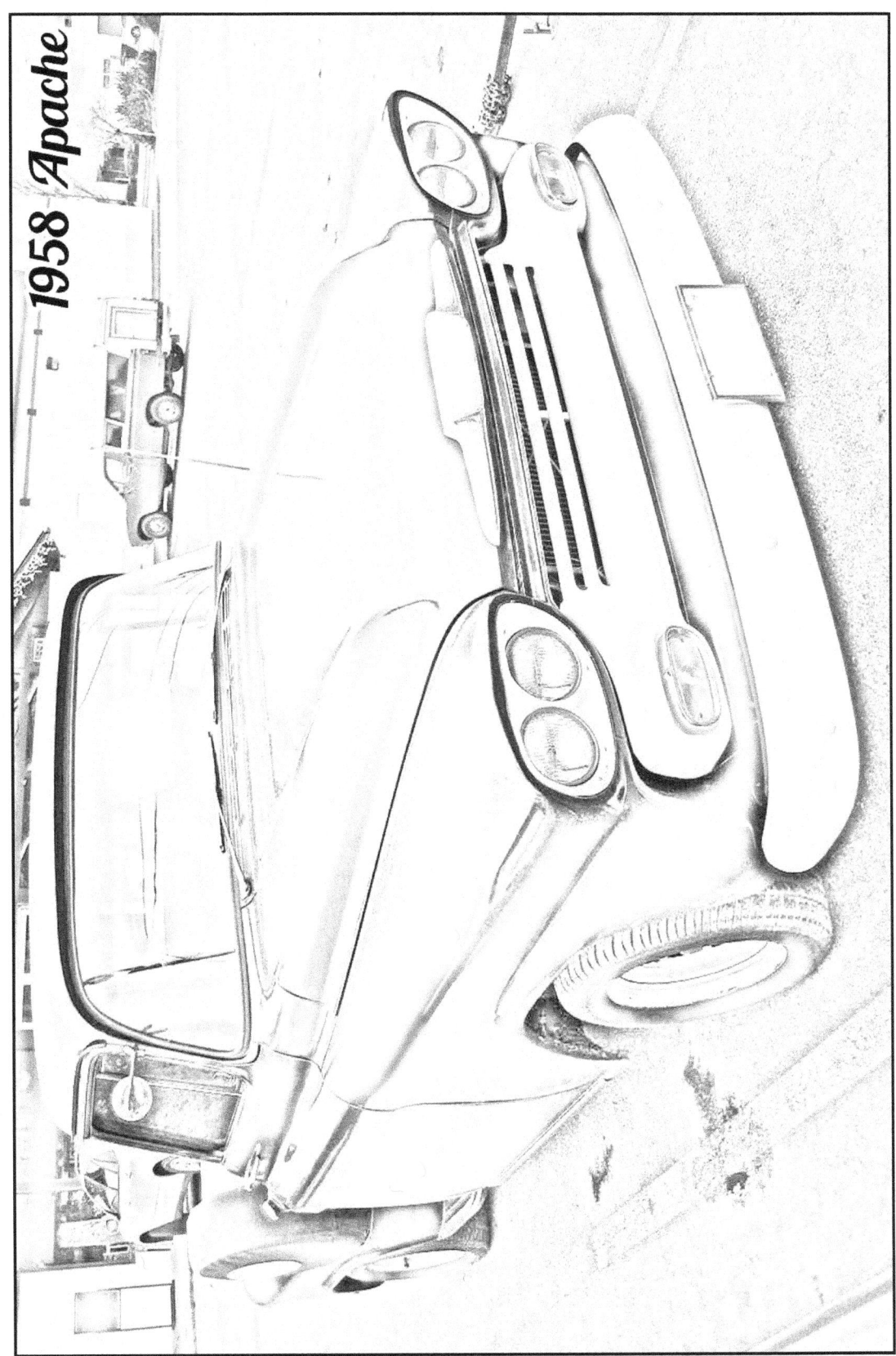

1958 Apache

1960 Corvette

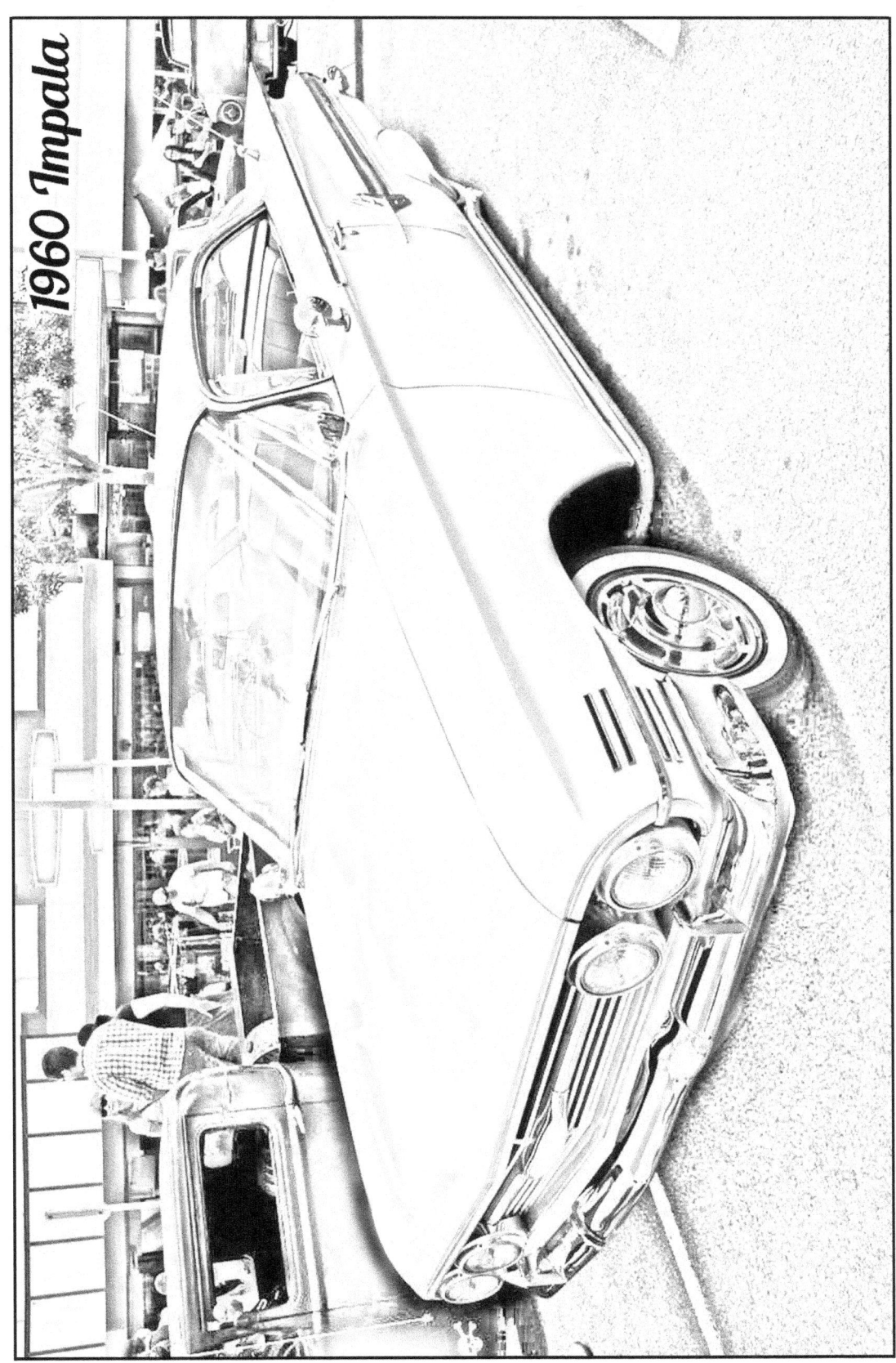

1960 Impala

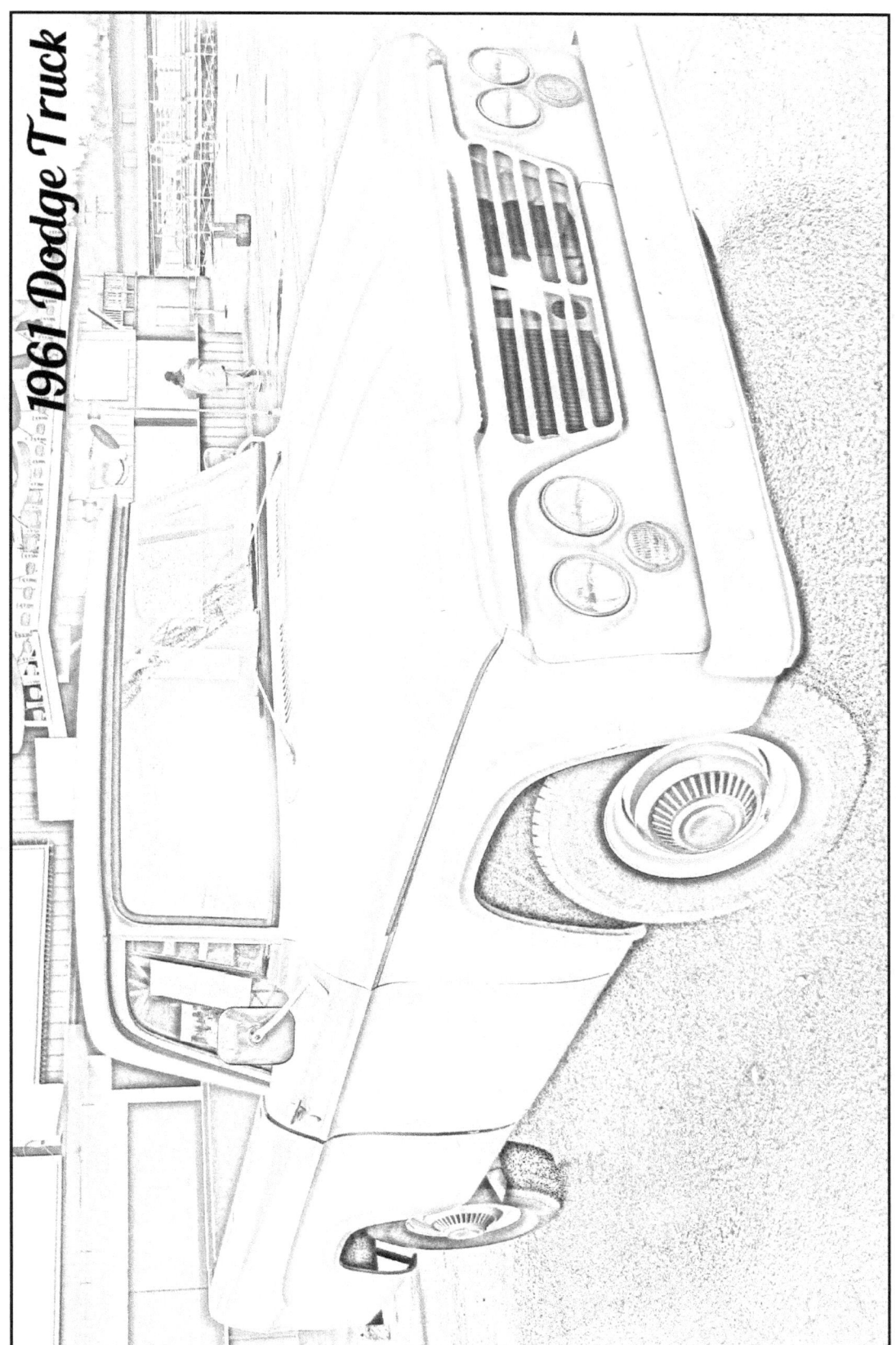

1961 Dodge Truck

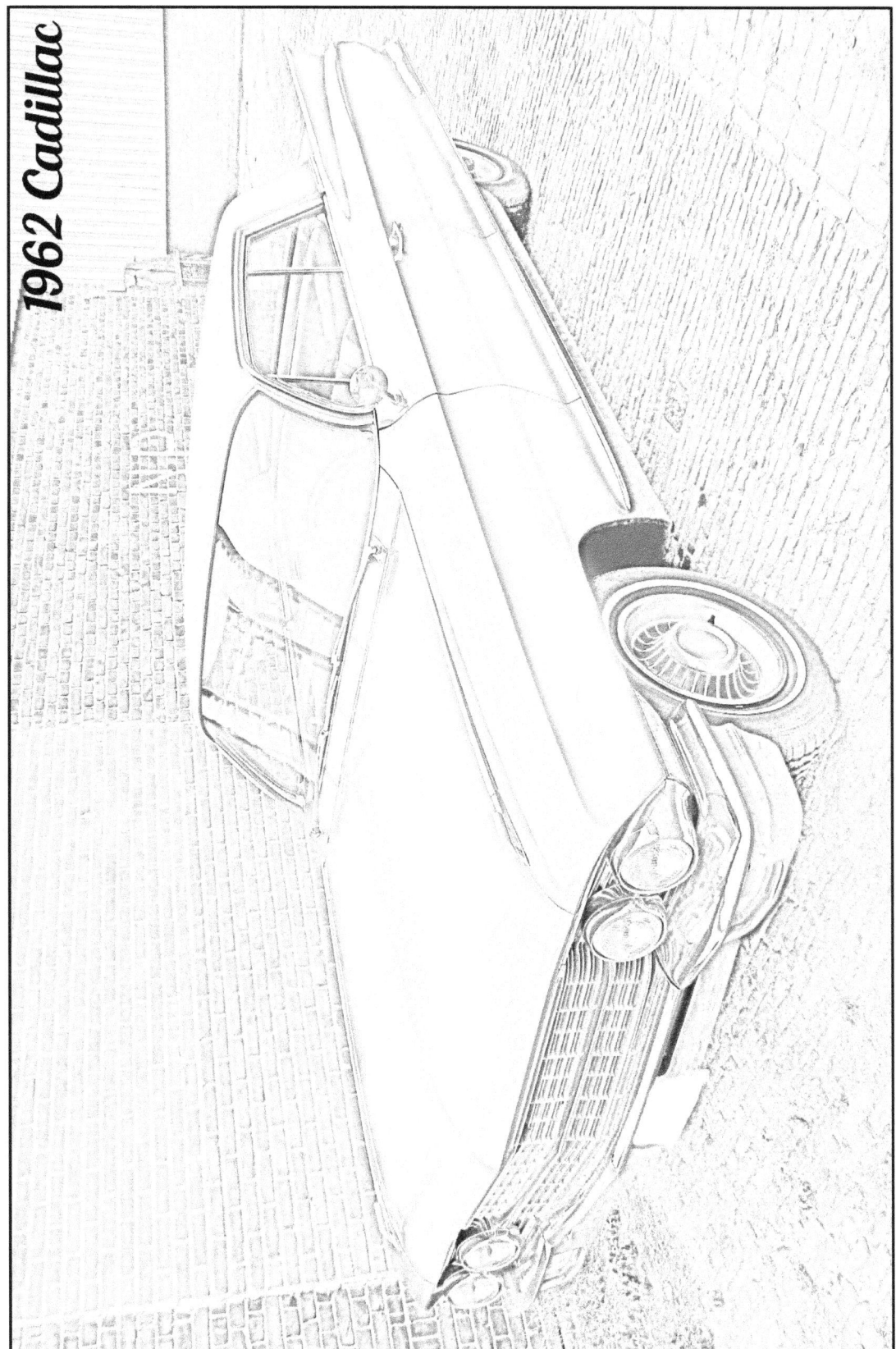

1962 Cadillac

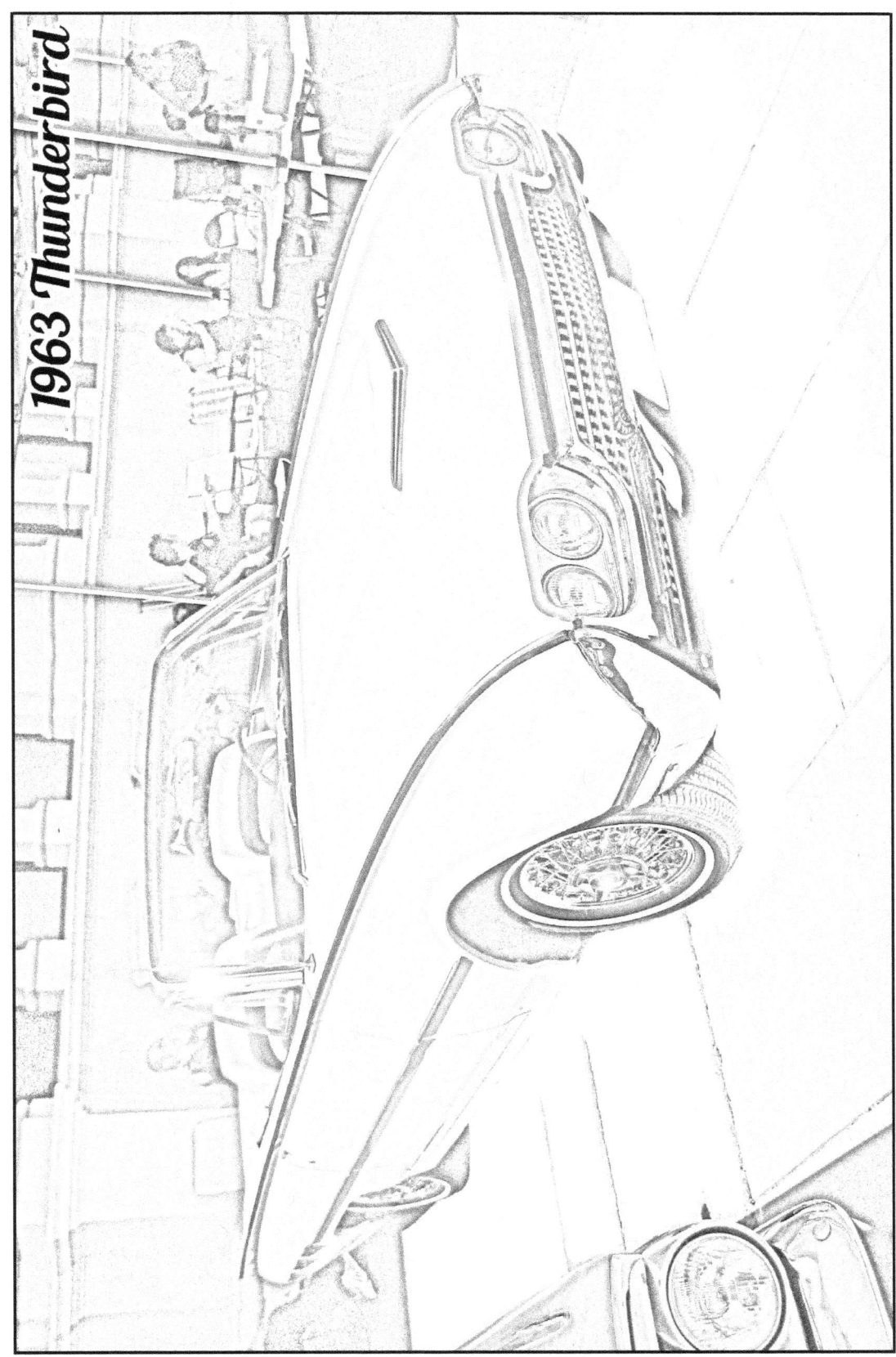

1963 Thunderbird

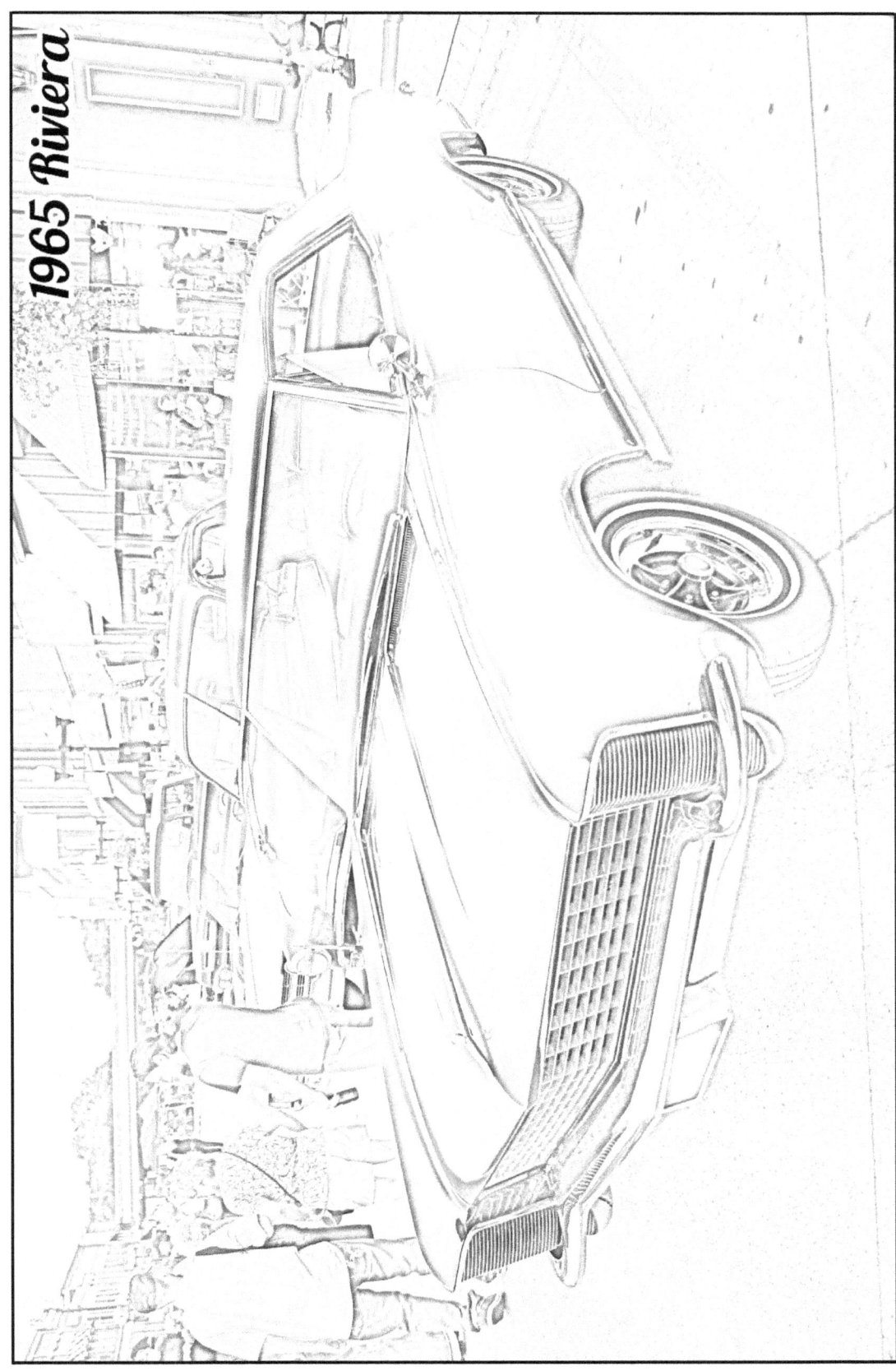

1965 Riviera

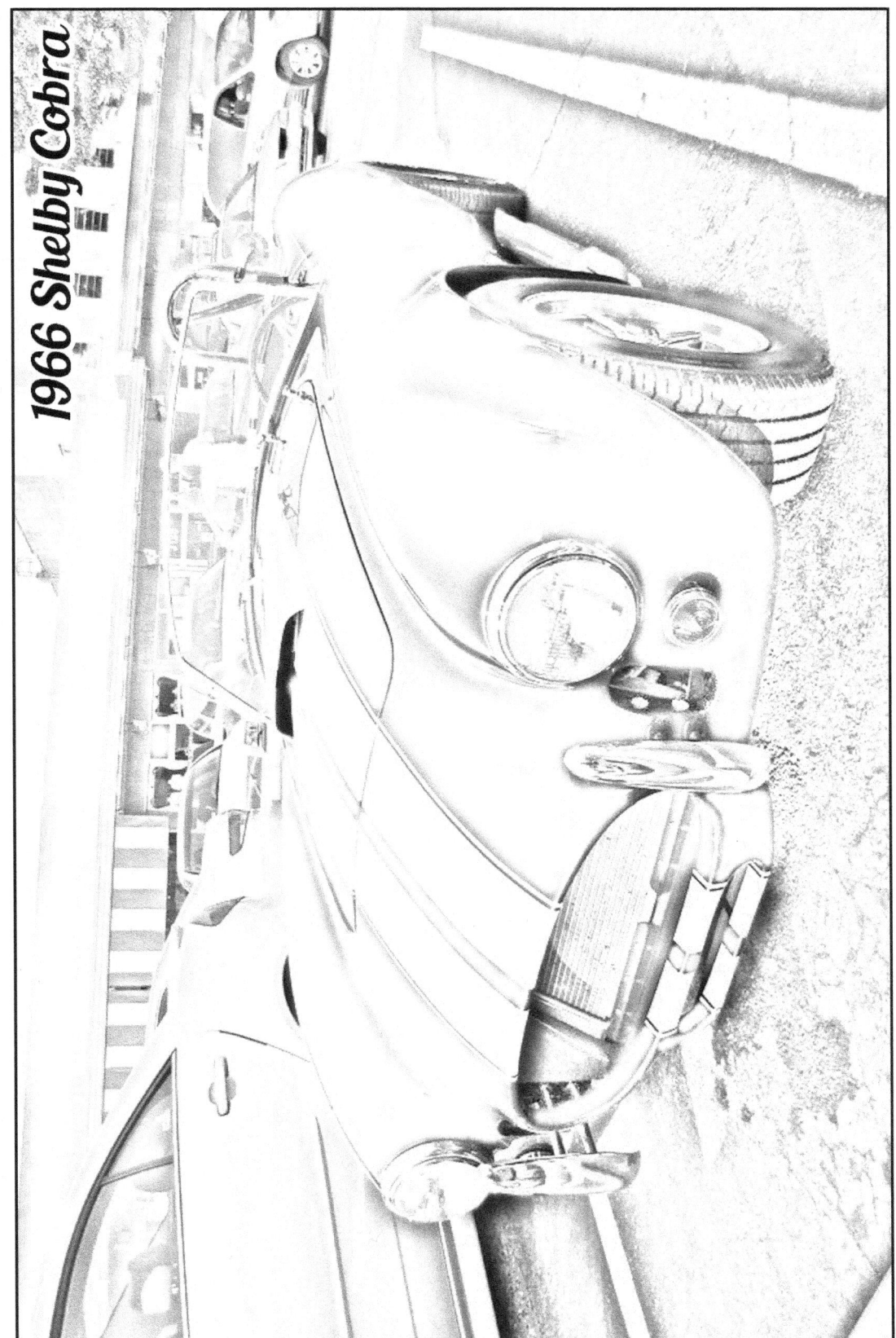

1966 Shelby Cobra

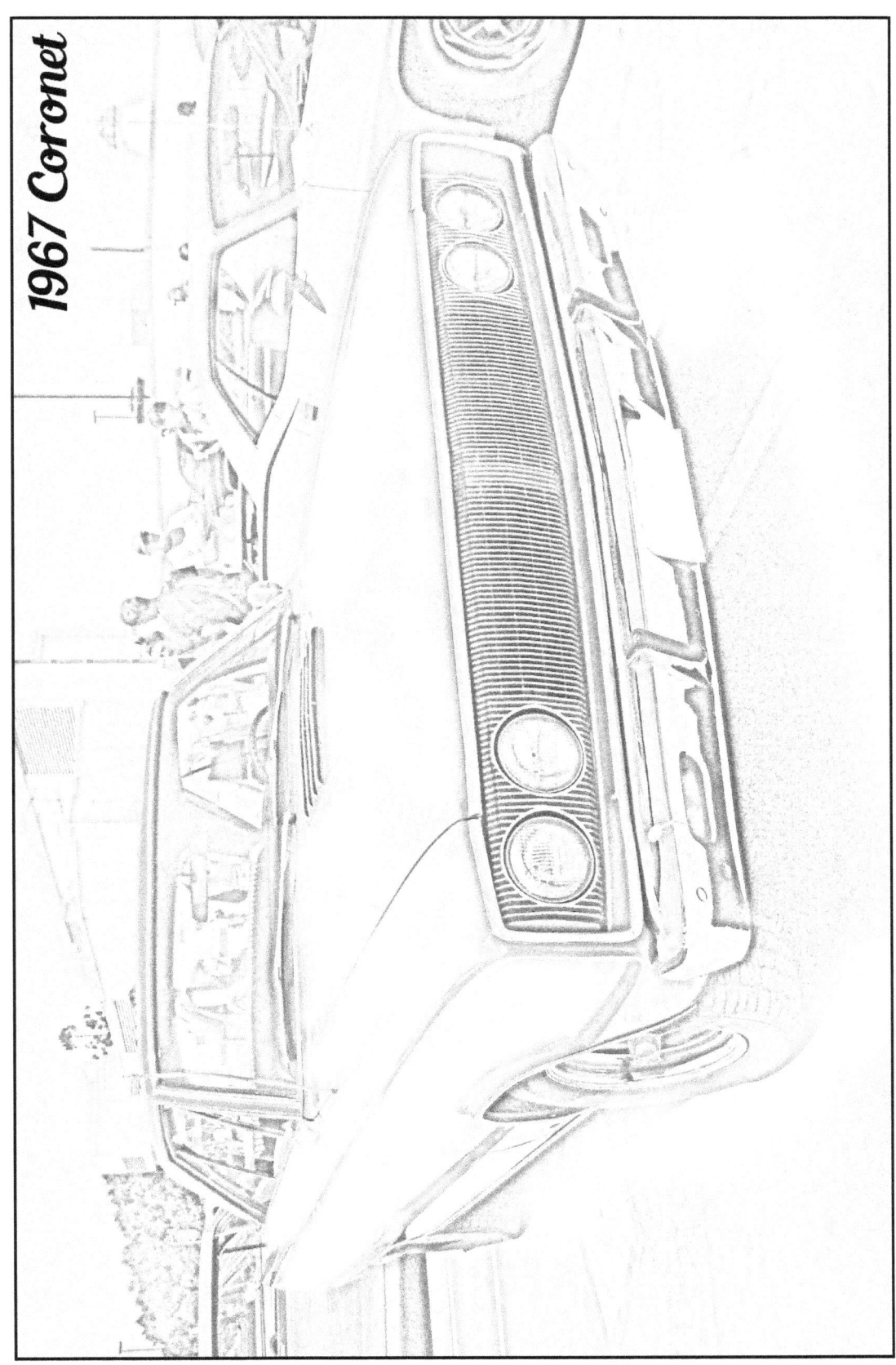

1967 Coronet

1967 Corvette

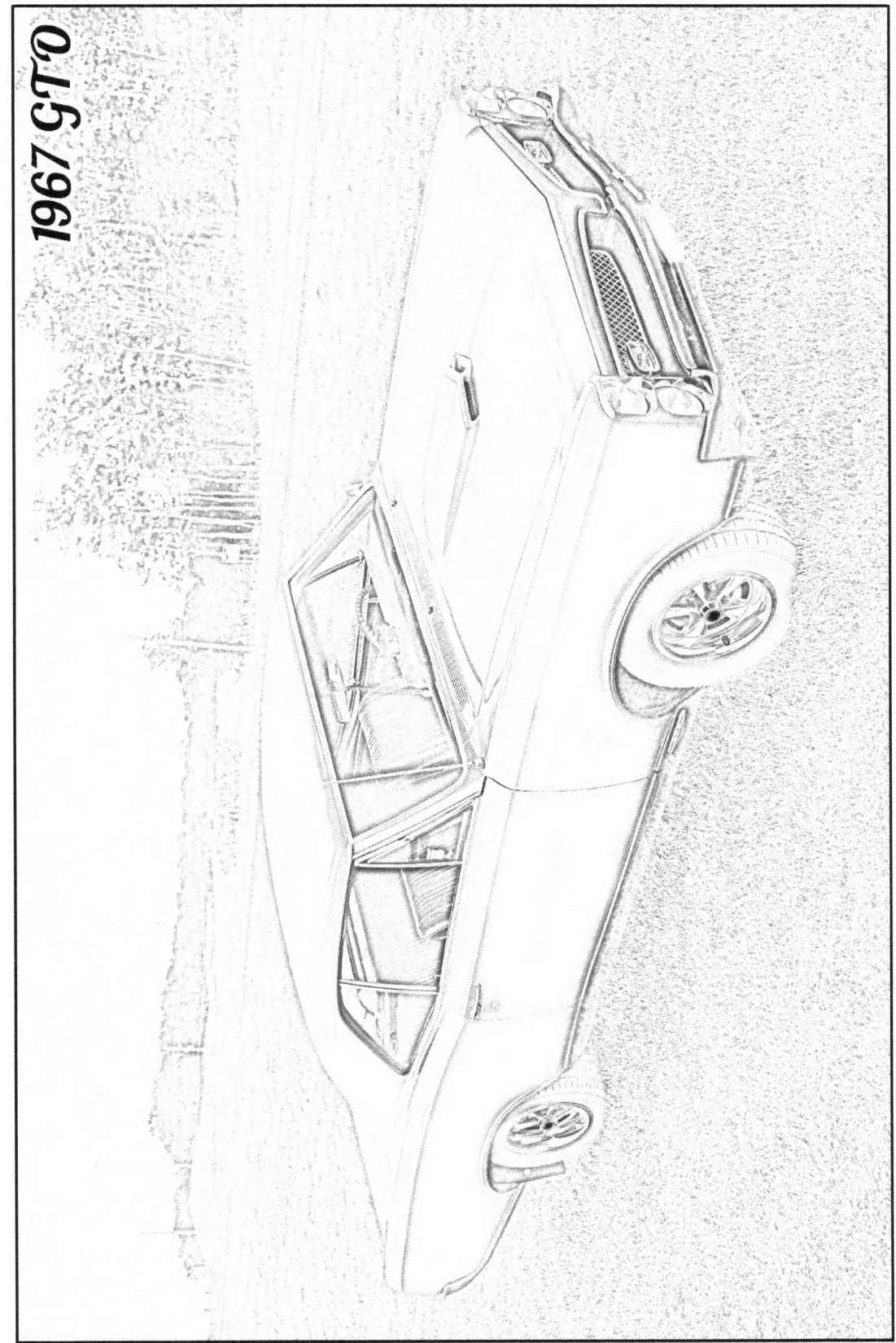

1967 GTO

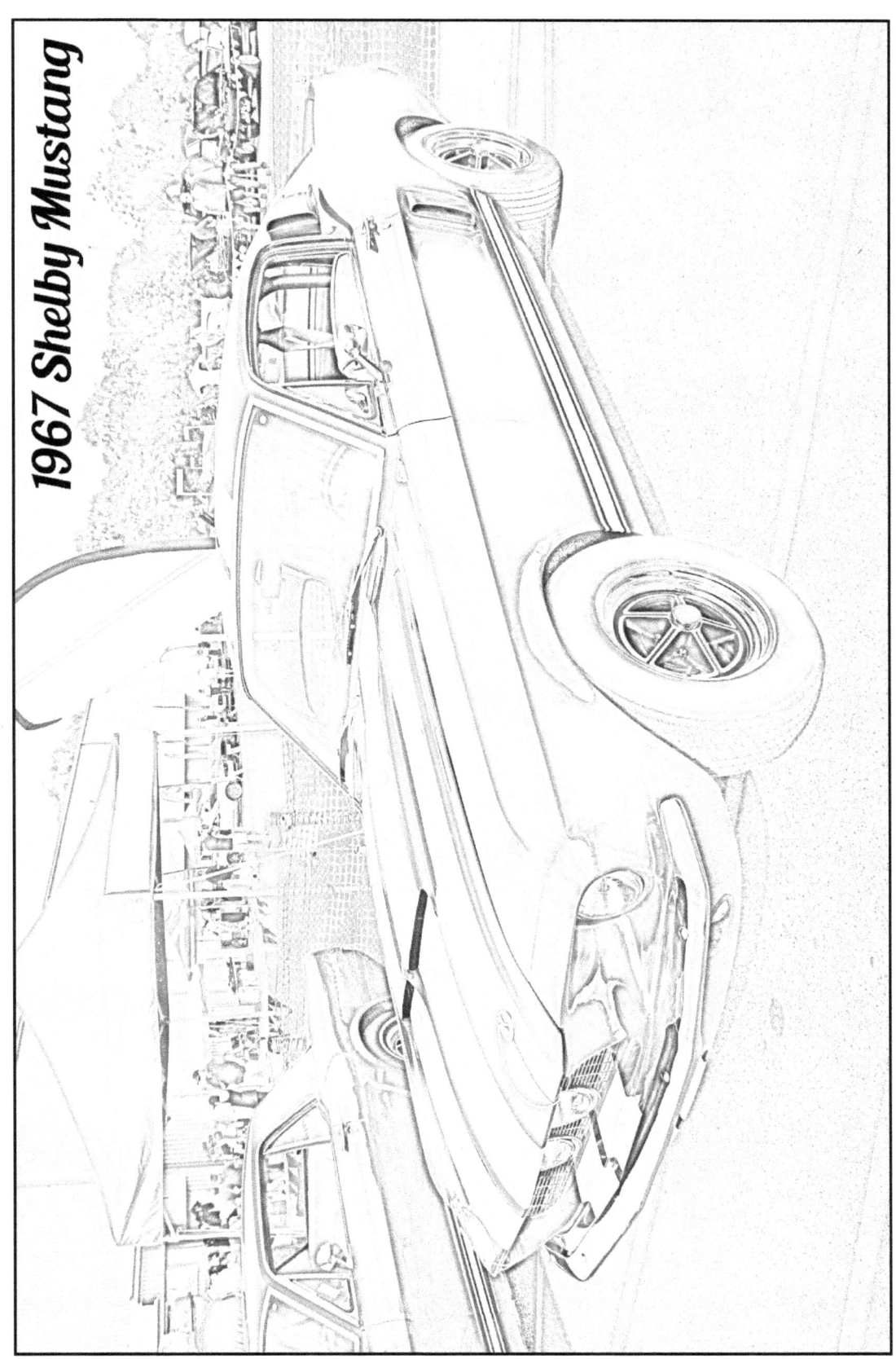

1967 Shelby Mustang

1969 Camaro

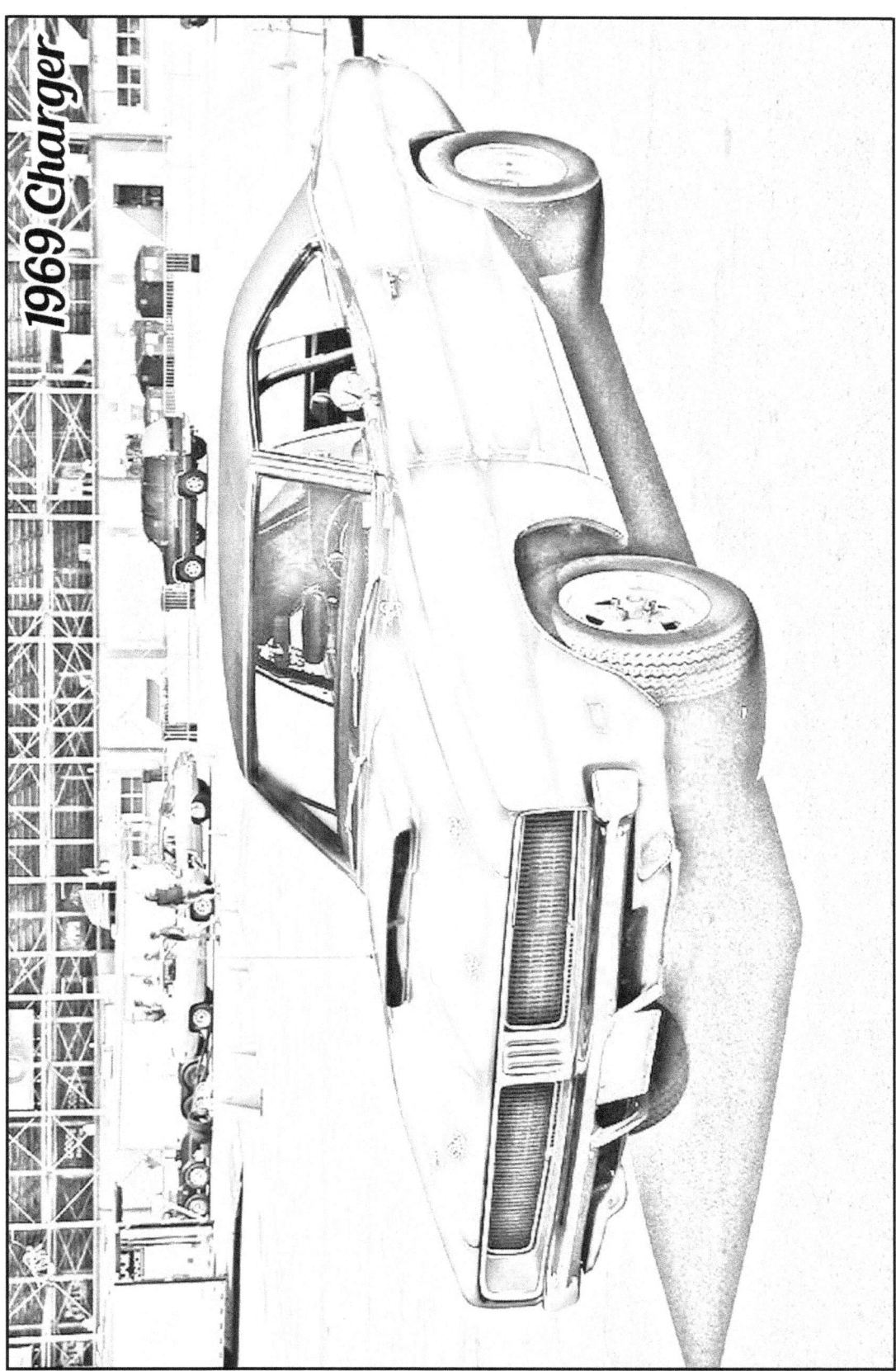

1969 Charger

1970 Super Bee

1970 Super Bird

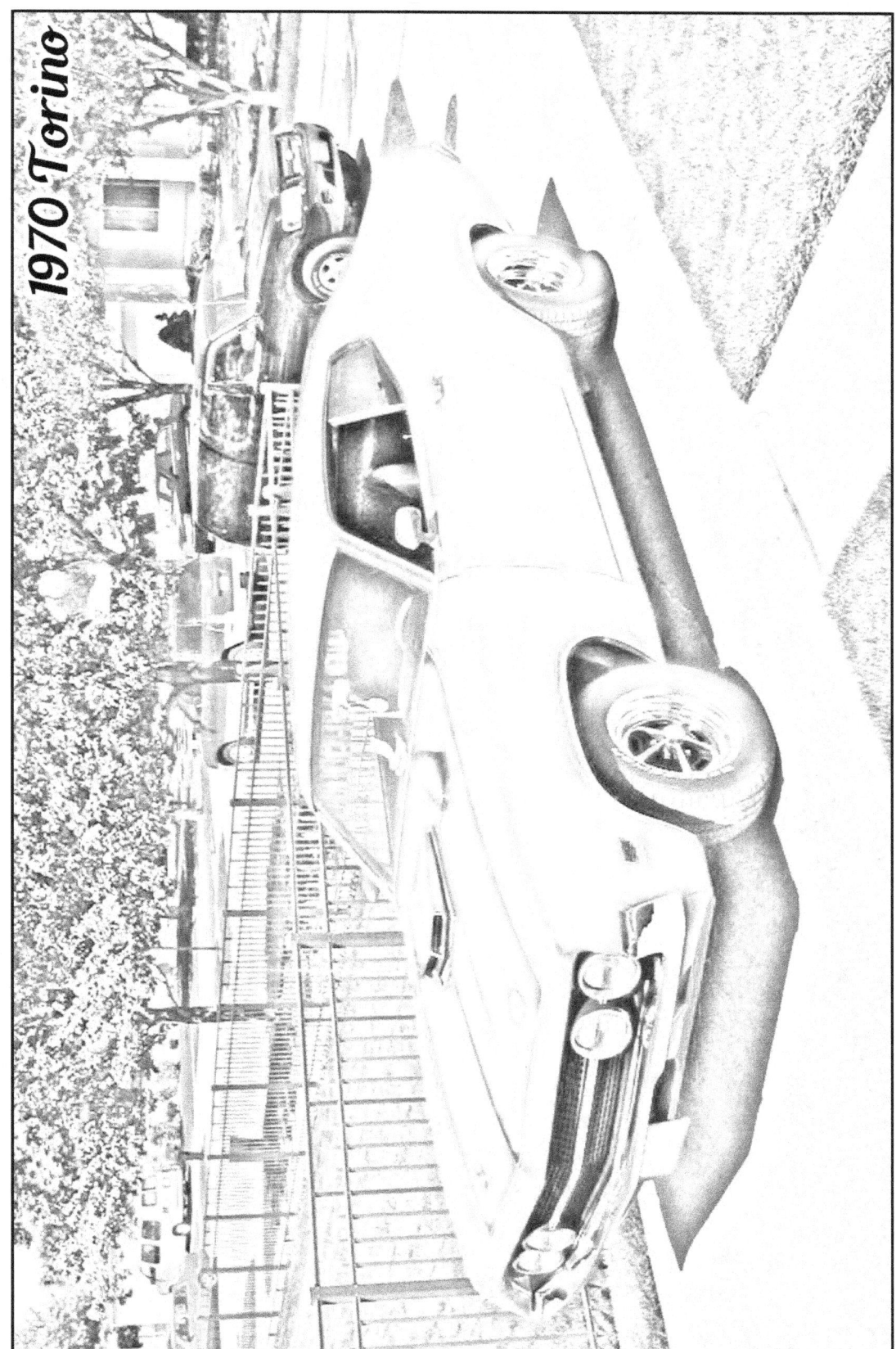

1970 Torino

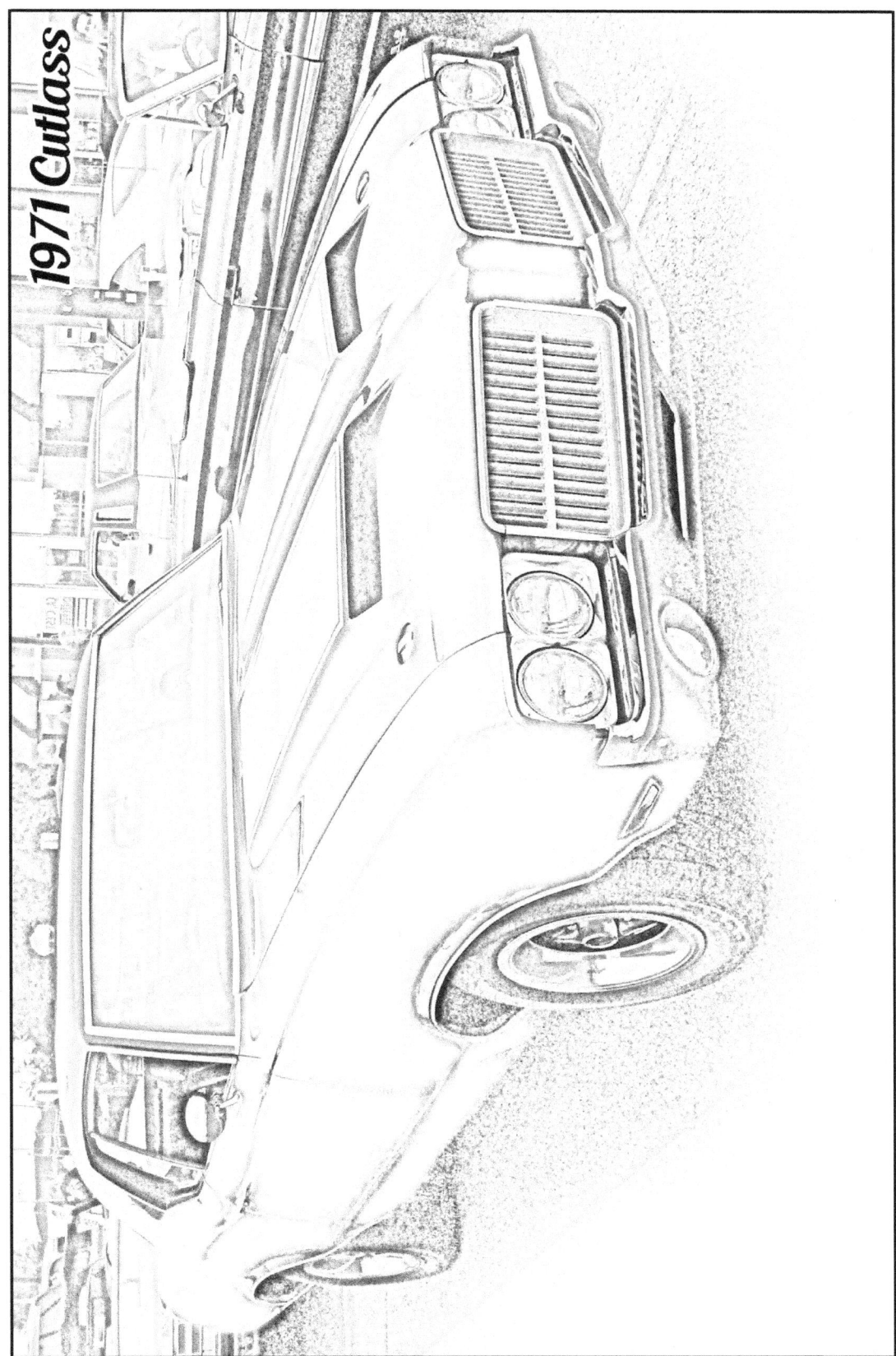

1971 Cutlass

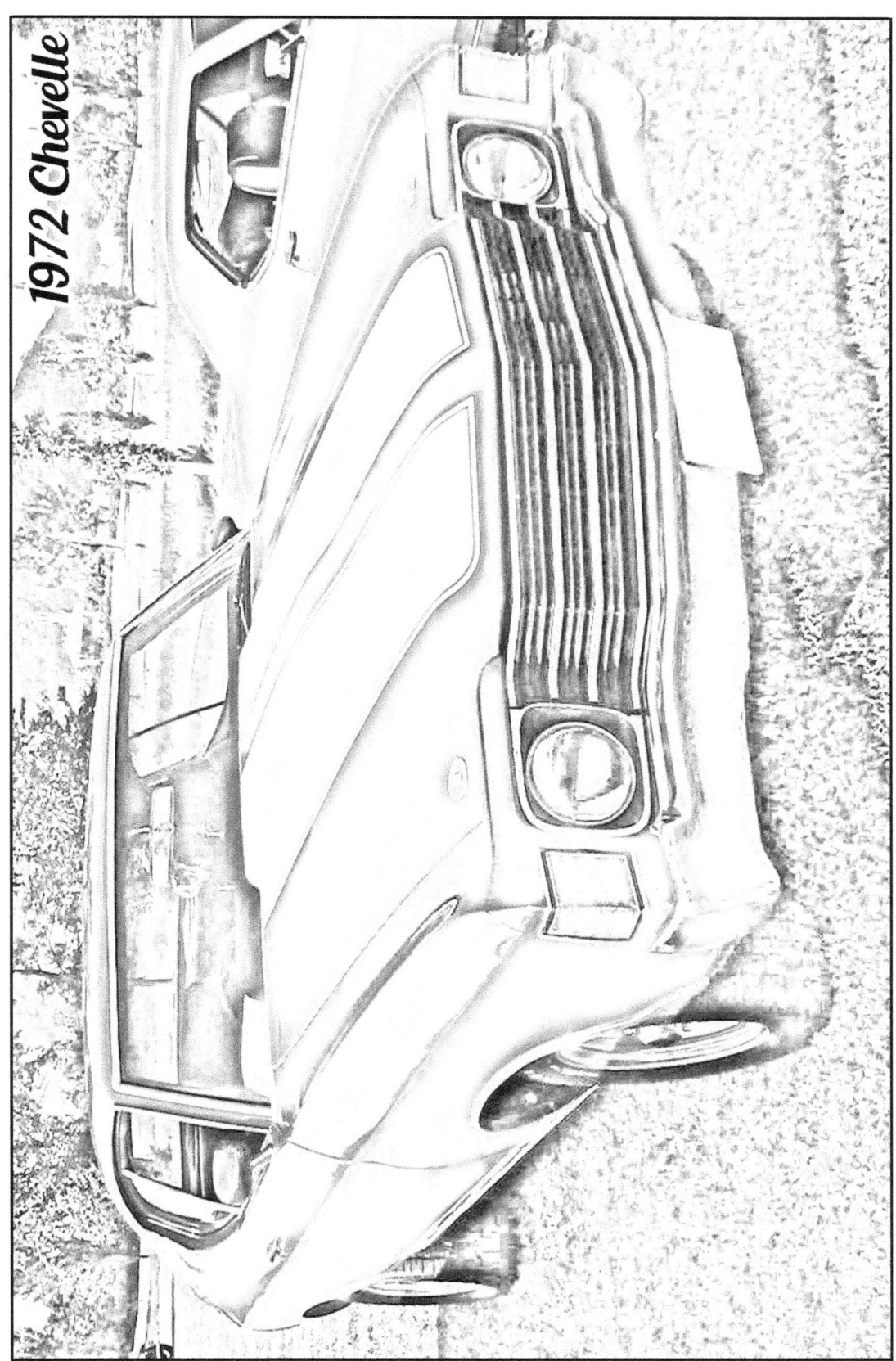

1972 Chevelle

1973 Camaro

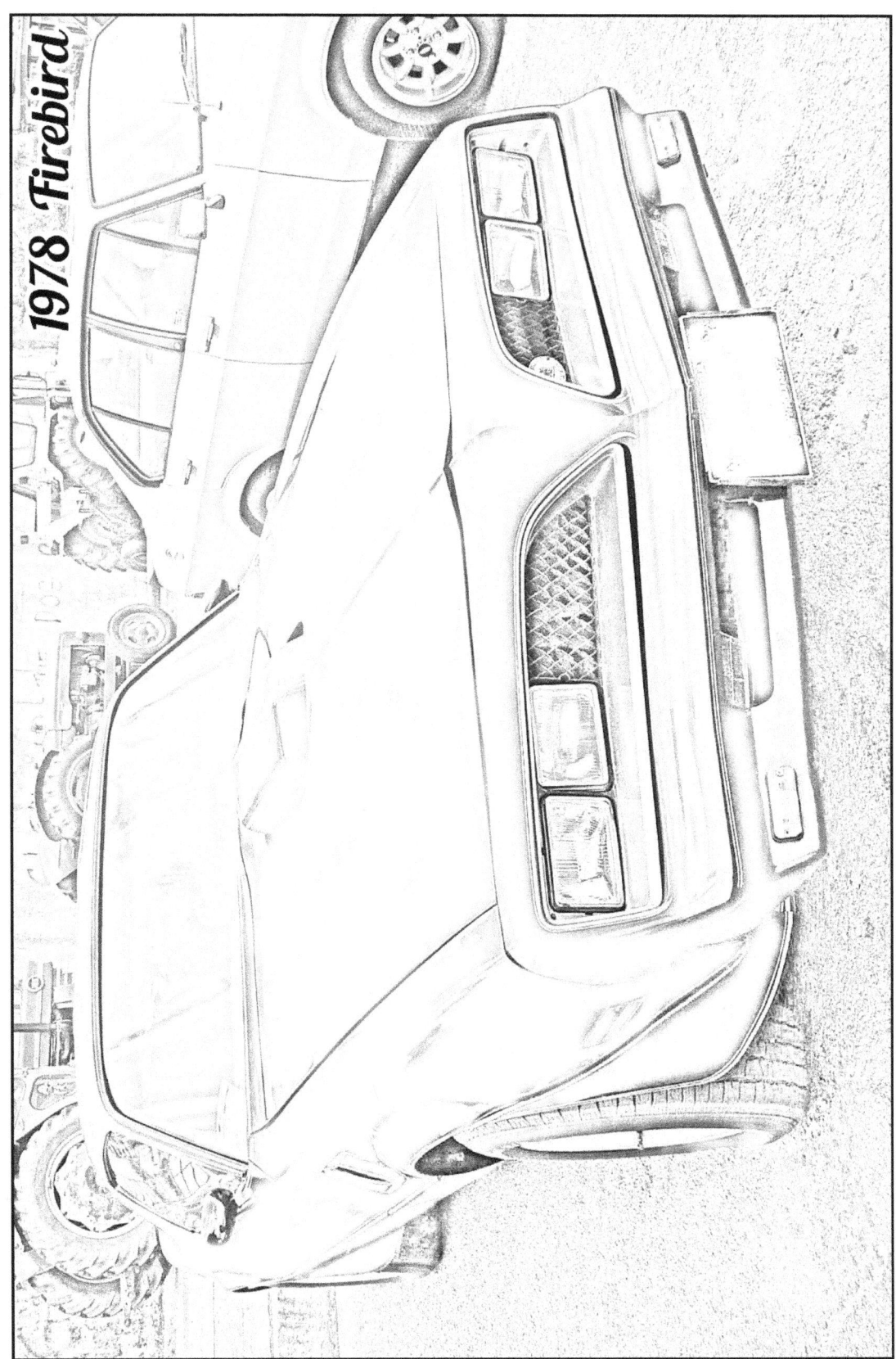

1978 Firebird